D1134183

PUFFINS

Colin Baxter Photography, Grantown-on-Spey, Scotland

PUFFINS

Atlantic puffins are perhaps the most instantly recognisable seabirds in their namesake ocean. They spend seven months or more each year entirely at sea, far from land. But when they return to their colonies in spring, their breeding finery is unmistakable. Multi-coloured beak, bright orange feet and crisp black-and-white plumage are their trademarks.

There are three species of puffins in the world. Two – the horned puffin and the tufted puffin – live only in the North Pacific. The Atlantic puffin (called simply 'puffin' for most of this book) is the world's smallest, most abundant puffin. It breeds around the rim of the North Atlantic, from the high Arctic, in Svalbard, to the fairly mild, humid islands in the Gulf of Maine, far to the south.

Within this large range, zoologists recognise three different Atlantic puffin types, or 'sub-species'. The commonest and most widespread of these has colonies from Maine to north-east Canada, in eastern Greenland, Iceland and Norway. Its population could be more than 10 million birds, with Iceland home to the biggest concentrations of all.

A slightly smaller type breeds from the Faroe Islands to France, including Britain and Ireland. It could number some 1.5 million birds. The third type is scattered in small numbers in Svalbard and north-east Greenland. Very little is known about these big, rare birds, which may have a world population of only a few thousand.

Colony at Ingólfshöfði, Iceland

Think about puffins, and you'll probably picture them at
a colony. For about four months, from spring until late summer, colonies
are the focus of puffin life. Some colonies have only a handful of birds.
Others are huge. Iceland is home to millions of pairs of breeding
puffins, making it the world's puffin capital.

◀ HAVING A STRETCH

Puffins are members of the auk family. All auks have bodies adapted to cope with the stresses of swimming and diving, including short, narrow wings that can be used like oars. Puffins have added their own variations to this theme, including smaller skulls and deep powerful bills. A puffin's bulk helps the bird to plunge and swim underwater, but also means that its wings have to work hard to keep it airborne.

SMART JACKET ▶

Many seabirds share the puffin pattern of dark plumage on wings and upper body and pale feathers on the underside. A white chest could help puffins, when seen from below, to be less obvious to fish. Dark feathers are tougher than light ones – useful for the wings. They are also good at absorbing heat. So a puffin's neat feather-scheme makes practical sense.

Puffin bills are made of the same material as human fingernails and toenails. New sheaths of this grow over a duller beak structure every spring. Tinted with pigments, these give the puffin its colours. Deep lines on the outer part of the bill give a rough pointer to age. Puffins with fewer than two bill 'grooves' are likely to be less than five years old. Two (like this bird) or more point to an adult. Beyond that, the age is anyone's guess. A three-groove bird, for example, could be younger than one with two-and-a-half grooves.

BILLING

When two puffins slap their beaks together in a quick-fire bout of 'billing', you can hear the noise several metres away. Mates use billing as an attention-grabbing greeting which demonstrates their ownership of a burrow area to other puffins. Birds trying to find a mate use billing in courtship – and may switch billing partners in mid-bout.

PUFFIN AMONG SEA CAMPION FLOWERS

Male and female puffins look alike, although in pairs you can sometimes see that females tend to be slightly smaller. This similarity may be because both sexes have a similar job to do in the breeding season. They have a fairly even share of the work of nesting, incubation of the single egg and chick rearing.

GATHERING NEST MATERIAL ▶

Puffin nests are often a simple scrape in soil at the end of a burrow, or in gravel under large rocks, lined with a few feathers and grasses. But on slopes where the soil can become waterlogged, gathering material to cushion the egg is vital work. Fresh grass is a popular choice. Large feathers can also attract a nester's attention. Puffins have an effect on vegetation in their colonies, both through the rain of nitrogen-rich droppings that they deposit (excellent fertiliser for some grasses and plants), and through trampling and digging.

TIME OUT

Colony life can be hectic. Courtship,
fighting, pair bonding, digging, egg
warming, food finding and chick feeding
are all part of it. So is trying to avoid
being caught by a predator. But when a
puffin finds time to rest you may see
a different side to its character. These
are long-lived birds, which may visit their
colonies as breeders for twenty years or
more. So each may experience the highs
and lows of colony life many times.
A summer when fish are hard to find will,
with luck, be followed by richer pickings
in the following year. A beakload of
young sandeels will give a good meal for
a growing puffin chick. But size matters,
and at times when better prey is scarce,
puffins may catch smaller, larval sandeels.
These have almost no food value.

◄ ALL MY OWN WORK

The majority of puffins around the North Atlantic breed in burrows. Although puffins can take over tunnels dug by rabbits, they are also perfectly able to construct their own burrow. The strong beak acts as a pickaxe, the clawed feet as scrapers and earthmovers. A young puffin pair may need to begin excavation a year or more before they can occupy a completed burrow. From entrance to nest chamber, this can stretch more than a human's arm-length. In many burrows, the chamber floor is slightly higher than the passage.

SNUG BELOW GROUND

A few centimetres of soil give the chick a roof, shielding it from wind, rain and strong sunlight. A tunnel lets it hear some sounds from above, and forms the supply line for parents bringing food. If all goes well, a young puffin can be cosy, entertained and well fed for the six weeks it spends in its nest.

BRINGING HOME THE CATCH

Locating shoals of fish within easy flying range of a colony can be difficult. A place that gives a good catch in the morning could yield nothing in the afternoon. But a successful fisher like this one must be wary. Its obvious beakful could attract the attention of food pirates, such as gulls and skuas.

LOADED ▶

A puffin only carries fish openly when it is feeding a youngster. At other times, it simply swallows the food it needs for itself. Backward-pointing spines on the roof of its mouth help to resist slippage and allow a bigger catch. But even these non-slip grips can't explain how some huge beakloads can be caught and held. The record catches (in Norway and Scotland) for Atlantic puffins both contained more than sixty small fry – a miracle of fish packing.

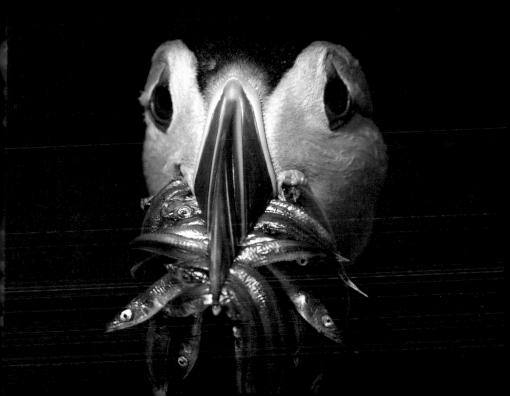

◄ PUFFIN CENTRAL

Sitting south of the Icelandic mainland, swept by strong currents and with deep water nearby, the Westmann Islands are a good fishing base for both people and puffins. The town on the island of Heimaey is a major fishing port. Many puffins burrow in slopes overlooking the town and harbour, and on other islands in the group. Together, they form the biggest puffin population in the world.

READY FOR TAKEOFF ►

Westmann Islanders probably know more about what a juvenile puffin looks like than just about anyone else. After it sheds the fluffy down, a small chick, a 'lundepisur', is like a small-beaked, monochrome version of its parents. Even its foot webs are fleshy grey.

RESCUE PATROL

When a six-week-old puffin leaves its nest to go to sea, it does so alone and at night, usually flying to the water. Some of the fledglings on Heimaey fly down into the town instead of out to sea. They may be attracted by the noise and lights. Groups of children go on patrol to rescue these confused birds. After putting them in cardboard boxes, children and parents take them early next morning for release at a beach out of town.

◀ THE BIG WHEEL

At many colonies, massed flights are part of the summer spectacle. Puffins often move from sea to land by first making a few circuits of their home area in a flock called a 'wheel'. This follows a broad track over the water, in over the land and back to sea again, with all birds moving in the same direction – like a school of fish. If possible, puffins fly with the wind behind them over the sea and against the wind (to slow them down) over burrow areas. Each puffin can use the wheel as a way of gaining extra protection against flying predators which get confused by big groups of prey.

LIFE ON THE OCEAN WAVES

Most of a puffin's life is spent at sea. Even in the breeding season, it will be on or over the water in search of fish for many of the daylight hours, and may spend the night roosting on the ocean. Through autumn, winter and early spring, puffins do not come ashore. They scatter widely over large areas, and are hard to spot amongst the waves.

OFF DUTY ▶

Rocks and hummocks can be good places for puffins to socialise or simply to relax. These 'club' areas can be where un-paired puffins first meet and begin courting prospective mates. They also provide useful lookout points at times of possible danger. Keeping feathers in good order is time-consuming, but necessary, and a puffin may spend many minutes using its bill to carefully smooth and arrange flight and body feathers, and taking oil from a gland at the top of its tail to waterproof them.

Fresh In

The ideal meal for a puffin chick
is a few chunky fish such as herring,
cod or sandeel. These give an oil-
and protein-rich food to boost growth.
To catch them, a parent needs to
plunge down a few metres below
the sea surface. Then, beating its
wings up and down for propulsion
and using its feet as a rudder, it can
travel fast beneath the waves. It looks
as if it is 'flying' underwater. Amazingly,
the puffin then uses the same
equipment when it surfaces to make
a fast move up and away to its colony.
But although small wings relative to
body size are a good idea below
water, they mean hard work in the
air, with rapid wing beats and high
energy consumption.

◀ TUFTED PUFFINS

Largest of the world's three puffin species, the tufted puffin also has the greatest geographical range. It breeds around the North Pacific, from Big Sur in California, through the Aleutian Islands and down to Hokkaido in Japan. It is commonest in Alaska, where the population is estimated in millions.

HORNED PUFFINS ▶

The horned puffin takes its name from the dark fleshy 'horn' that sits above each eye as a breeding season decoration. But the sheer size of its bill is equally striking. Horned puffins breed only around the North Pacific where they share about half their range with tufted puffins.

◄ LOOKING BACK,
  LOOKING FORWARD

Atlantic puffins have fared well in some parts
of their range, but had problems in others.
The Icelandic population seems to be stable,
while numbers in Britain have held steady or
increased. In the Lofoten Islands of Arctic
Norway – still a major breeding area – puffins
have continued to decline and suffer chick
starvation more than thirty years after
industrial-scale fishing for young herring there
stopped. Such exploitation and the risk of oil
pollution is still a threat in other places, while
the effect of rising sea temperature at a time of
global warming is uncertain. Many of the fish
that puffins eat thrive in cold water. So warmer
conditions, linked to human use of fossil fuels,
could pose a serious threat. The future health
of puffins will depend on wise conservation of
resources, both at sea and on land.

First published in Great Britain in 2001 by Colin Baxter Photography Ltd,
Grantown-on-Spey, PH26 3NA, Scotland
www.colinbaxter.co.uk
Reprinted 2003

A CIP Catalogue record for this book is available from the British Library.
ISBN 1-84107-086-6   *Colin Baxter Gift Book Series*   Printed in Hong Kong

Photographs © 2001: Colin Baxter: front cover, 1,2,4,5,7,22,25 Laurie Campbell: back cover, 8,16,30,31,32
Kenneth Day: 17   Mark Hamblin: 11,13,26,27 Sigurgeir Jonasson:18,19,20,21 Stephen Krasemann (NHPA): 28,29
Jean-Louis Le Moigne (NHPA): 23   Neil McIntyre: 6   Richard Packwood: 10,12   Allan G. Potts (Bruce Coleman): 14
Andy Rouse (NHPA): 9   Kenny Taylor: 15   David Woodfall (NHPA): 24